Capyboppy

written and illustrated by

BILL PEET

CLARION BOOKS
AN IMPRINT OF HARPERCOLLINS*PUBLISHERS*
BOSTON   NEW YORK

NOTE

A capybara is a real animal. It is the largest existing rodent and looks something like a giant guinea pig, to which it is related. Normally the capybara lives near the rivers and lakes of South America, but this one lived with the Peet family.

TO CAPY

Printed in Vietnam

ISBN 0-395-24378-5 Reinforced Edition
ISBN 0-395-38368-4 Sandpiper Paperbound Edition

23 RRDA 40 39 38 37 36 35

Since early childhood my son Bill has been fascinated by the wild creatures living around the Los Angeles and southern California area. His room has always been part zoo and part museum with a bed sandwiched in between. Over the years this bedroom zoo has included tarantulas, praying mantises, scorpions, turtles, frogs, horned toads, lizards, kangaroo rats, pack rats, and a variety of harmless snakes.

After observing these creatures for a while Bill always set them free in the general area where he'd found them, only to return with another variety of small animal. So the zoo was forever changing.

When Bill entered college to major in the natural sciences the long hours of study left little time for creature collecting. Early one spring the zoo had dwindled to its lowest population in years — a mere pair of tarantulas. It was then he decided on a spectacular new addition.

"I know where I can get a boa at a bargain," Bill said one day.

This brought an immediate storm of protest from my wife
Margaret, our younger son Steve, and me. We knew that Bill
was sometimes careless and left a lid slightly ajar on one of his
glass cases. There was the time when a king snake came slith-
ering out to the kitchen, and one afternoon a tarantula was
found stumbling about on a bedspread. These creatures were
easily captured and returned to their quarters, so there was
no problem.

However, if a big boa should escape and take a tour of the house that would be another matter. We had our three cats to worry about. Three hopelessly spoiled cats who were fussy about their food and spent much of their time drowsing upon chairs and sofas or stretched out on a rug.

Spoiled or not we were extremely fond of them and I shivered at the thought of the giant snake reclining on a sofa with three cat-sized bumps in his middle.

"It's only a small boa," Bill explained.

"Small boas grow into big boas," I argued.

"All right," Bill said, "I'll forget about the boa. Now how about a capybara?"

"A capybara? Fine! Fine!" we quickly agreed. "That's much more like it."

We had read about capybaras and seen pictures of them. They are the world's largest species of rodent, sometimes reaching a weight of two hundred pounds.

These animals are vegetarians and live in swamps or along riverbanks in the South American jungles. Their thick bodies are covered with coarse brown hair. They have no tail. Their feet are partly webbed and they are good swimmers. When in captivity the capybara is known to be very friendly.

Bill lost no time in contacting a wild-animal importer to put in his order for one capybara. That was in the middle of March. One afternoon in early April Bill came wheeling happily home in his jeep with his new rodent friend seated beside him.

The instant the jeep pulled to a stop in front of the house the capybara was out the car door, and he came waddling up the walk, as if he understood that this was his new home. Margaret, Steve, and I rushed out to greet him but he passed us by without a glance, twitching his tiny mouse ears and making a bird-like "tweetle-tweet" sound. After taking a few nibbles at the ivy he hopped onto the porch, then "tweetle-tweeted" on in the front door.

He paused in the entry hall for a brief look around, then headed into the family room where the cats were drowsing on the love seat. At the sound of the "tweetle-tweet" the cats suddenly sat up. Perhaps they expected to see a bird.

But when they spied the huge no-tailed mouse they were horrified. They exploded off the love seat "kitty-boom!" and went streaking away to the living room.

The capybara hardly noticed them. He followed his sensitive nose straight for the kitchen to the three bowls of cat food which had hardly been touched. Vegetarian though he was, the capybara seemed to enjoy the cat food. He finished off one bowl after another while the bewildered cats watched at a safe distance.

What a shock it must have been to see the old cat-and-mouse game turned completely topsy-turvy. However, the cats hadn't seen anything yet. The big rodent was only five or six weeks old, and was just beginning to grow.

After finishing off the cat food he put away a heaping big bowl of oats and barley. Then the capy began exploring the house with all four of us trailing after him, curious to see how our jungle creature would take to his new surroundings.

We followed his cheery "tweetle-tweet" as he wandered in and out of the rooms, circling behind chairs, snooping under beds, and exploring every closet.

All at once we realized he was doing much more than snooping, he was sampling things for taste. To the capybara everything was edible until proven otherwise. A few quick nips and a shoe was beyond repair, "crunch!" and a wicker chair seat began to unravel, "chomp!" and a handbag strap flew apart. This was proof enough that the capy was not the ideal household pet so we promptly escorted him out to the backyard.

If we had planned the yard for the visitor from the Amazon jungle it couldn't have been more ideal. There was a swimming pool with a border of broad-leaved tropical plants, and on beyond was a sloping bank overgrown with a dense tangle of trees and shrubs; and our jungle was completely fenced in.

We watched anxiously as he sniffed the tropical plants, certain that they were doomed to the very last leaf. But after a few nibbles the capy lost interest and waddled out onto the lawn.

He found the lawn much more to his taste and he settled
down to graze, his large rodent teeth clipping off the grass
about an inch from the ground as neatly and evenly as a lawn
mower. A mower with built-in grasscatcher that left no wheel
tracks. The lawn area was small and Capy could have finished the mowing job in half an hour if he hadn't been dis-
tracted by the glitter of sunlit water. And he headed for the
pool.

17

For a moment he teetered awkwardly on the edge then toppled in "ker plosh!" Once in the water, Capy was surprisingly graceful. His broad webbed feet propelled him along in a smooth easy glide with his eyes, ears, and nose skimming over the surface.

After one leisurely cruise around the pool he hauled himself out. Swimming all alone wasn't much fun. Capy needed
a few playmates and a bit of competition to show what a
truly fine swimmer he was.

Bill and Steve were gone during the week to their summer jobs, but on the weekends when friends came to join them for a swim Capy was always in the thick of the action. The excitement of the shouting, splashing teenagers and small-fry brought out the show-off in the big rodent. He seemed to be everywhere, dodging in and out and under flying arms and legs and swim fins.

Nobody could outdo Capy when it came to swimming underwater, but then he had all the natural equipment such as self-sealing nostrils and ears, plus two pairs of swim fins, and he circled the pool time after time before bobbing to the surface for air.

When at last the weary waterlogged swimmers gave up, Capy gave up too. He joined his friends in the sun, adding a few of his own "tweetle-tweets" to the general conversation. For all the capybara knew he was a teenager too, and a full-fledged member of our family.

After a full day of eating and swimming, Capy joined us
for the evening in the family room while we read or watched
television. He took his place on the love seat with his head
on Margaret's lap while three miserably jealous cats prowled
in the background.

There he remained without stirring, except for an occasional twitch of an ear, until it was time to carry him off to his bed in the garage. This was Bill's job; after all it was his rodent. And it was a struggle all the way with Capy kicking and squealing like a spoiled little pig. But then Capy *was* getting a bit spoiled.

As soon as Margaret gave him the special pet name "Capy-boppy" I knew the spoiling was well underway. His expressions of pleasure so delighted her that she was constantly thinking of new ways to make Capy happy.

His day began with a shower. Margaret turned on a fine warm spray in the stall shower and left Capy there while she prepared breakfast.

He flopped down on the slippery tile floor to go wriggling and rolling around on his back, tweetling joyfully all the while. Then after being fluff-dried with a beach towel he galloped off to the kitchen for a heaping bowl of oats and barley.

To Capy there was nothing quite so wonderful as a graham cracker. The flavor was irresistible. Margaret taught him to sit up and beg for them, and before long she had him walking on his hind legs all around the kitchen in pursuit of this very special treat.

Another of Capy's special treats was a good back scratching, and a long-handled backscratcher, a souvenir of old Chinatown, at last became useful. As Margaret worked the tiny wooden hand briskly up and down his back, the capybara's hair began to rise. Pretty soon every single hair stood straight out, and from a rear view Capy resembled an enormous seedpod with a pair of mouse ears.

During that first month our big jungle rodent had grown
accustomed to lots of attention, and if he was left to himself
in the yard for too long a time he called to us with a plain-
tive "tweetle-tweeeeet!"

One afternoon Capy came to visit me in my studio above
the garage. "Clumpity clump clump," he struggled to the
top of the stairs. Then came the persistent scratching at the
door until I finally let him in. I watched intently as he went
nosing his way around the cluttered room sniffing at the
jumbles of books, stacks of old magazines, and the hodge-
podge of paper and art materials. The only thing he found of
interest was a grease pencil which he promptly ate.

One grease pencil was no great loss. But when he began
staring at some drawings tacked on the wall, there was cause
for alarm. They were finished illustrations for a book I had
been working on since early spring. If the drawings happened to suit his taste he could eat a month's work in less than
a minute.

As much as I enjoyed Capy's company the risk was too
much, and after a brief but lively skirmish I managed to push
him out onto the stairway, and rudely shut the door behind
him.

I had lost a lot of working time since the rodent's arrival. Much of this time was spent watching him out of pure fascination. Then at frequent intervals during the day, I left the drawing board to check the gate between the house and the garage to be sure it was closed and latched. We had posted two notices on the gate in extra large print, "PLEASE KEEP GATE CLOSED," and "BEWARE OF CAPYBARA." Nevertheless, one day someone left the gate standing wide open and Capy was gone!

In a panic Margaret and I rushed out to the street. She
called "Capyboppy! Capyboppy!" toward the brush-covered
hills just below, while I raced up and down the block peering
over fences and between houses. But there was no answering
"tweetle-tweet" and not a sign of Capy. For all we knew he
might have been gone for an hour and might be miles away.
Our only hope was to drive slowly along the roads that went
winding down through the hills, asking everyone we met if
they had seen a big brown hairy thing with mouse ears and
no tail. So we rushed back to the house and leaped in the
car. Then just as we pulled out of the driveway Margaret
cried, "There he is! There's Capy!!"

Capy was sitting on the front porch staring at the door, patiently waiting to be let in. We hoped he'd come back because he missed us. But then he might have been thinking of graham crackers or a good backscratching. Or perhaps he was eager to get on with the new project he had going in the backyard.

This new project was a mudwallow. He had discovered a bare spot on the lawn and after a dip in the pool the dripping wet Capy kept rolling over and over on the spot until he had himself a sticky-icky quagmire.

Between the mudwallowing and the swimming, the pool was rapidly turning a deep chocolate brown. Unless something was done soon we would have the only swamp with a diving board and ladder.

The solution to this sticky problem proved to be a truck-tire innertube floating in the pool. It covered Capy's quagmire exactly, and we left the befuddled rodent staring gloomily at the huge rubber doughnut. I had no sooner settled down to the drawing board when Margaret shouted from below, "Come look at Capy!"

Capy had plunked himself down smack in the center of the innertube. There he sat in stubborn defiance. If he couldn't have his mudwallow, at least he was determined to have the last word.

This little show of stubbornness was only the beginning. The capybara was getting more headstrong by the day, which seemed to go along with his increasing size. He was growing at an alarming rate. He ate his way through June and July, and by early August he had just about tripled his size.

As big as he was, Capy still spent the evenings with us lounging on the love seat beside Margaret. But it wasn't quite the same. He was getting a little too smart for us. When he figured it was getting close to his bedtime he would suddenly leap to the floor and go galloping away down the hall.

We set out after him on a helter-skelter chase in and out through the bedrooms. When we thought we had him cornered he would slip through our grasp, dodge between our legs, and go charging off to another part of the house. Sometimes it took all four of us to round up the elusive Capy.

Once Capy was captured there was still the problem of hauling the seventy-five pound, kicking, squealing rodent out to the garage. At the rate he was growing he would soon have the edge on us, so for a while we tried leaving him in the backyard until bedtime. But Capy was not to be ignored and he kept squealing and scratching at the back door until we let him in and we were right back into the same old hectic routine. What Capy needed was a pen.

By this time Bill was done with his summer job and he spent a few days building a sturdy pen of two-by-fours and heavy wire fencing, with a packing box for a shelter. As soon as the pen was finished Bill took off in his jeep on a month-long camping trip in Mexico, leaving the capybara situation in pretty good shape — or at least so it seemed.

There was still the tricky problem of luring the reluctant rodent back into his pen at the end of the day. He couldn't be tempted with graham crackers. By this time he'd had his fill of them. Now the best bait was a fistfull of tender green grass. Capy kept the lawn so neatly trimmed that there was barely a nibble here and there, and he would do most anything for one good mouthful.

So with sacks and scissors Margaret and I went grass collecting in the surrounding hills every few days to make sure there was always an ample supply on hand. The grass was used strictly as bait, just a bit at a time, and Capy was always left in his pen squealing for more.

Then one Sunday afternoon we weakened. Capy's dreary mood got the better of us and we tried cheering him up with a feast, a heaping sackful of the precious green grass. Steve had brought a young friend to visit the capybara that day, seven-year-old Tommy Hall. The boy was so fascinated with our big rodent that we let him do the feeding while we watched, expecting Capy's spirits to rise with every mouthful. But there were no cheery "tweetle-tweets" of pleasure. He chewed the grass in sullen silence.

Then without warning Capy suddenly leaped at Tommy
and nipped him on top of the head! The boy screamed in
pain! At the same instant Steve let go with a furious kick
that sent the capybara sprawling into the pool.

Tommy's T-shirt was spattered with blood as Margaret and
Steve rushed him into the house. I was too stunned to move.
All I could do was stare helplessly after them, then back at
the pool where the capy was floundering on the bottom.

By the time I could get my legs to carry me in the back
door, the others were out the front door and in the car starting
off for the Valley Emergency Hospital.

As they pulled out of the driveway Margaret called out to
me, "Keep an eye on Capy!" and I returned for another look
into the depths of the pool, fearful of what I might find.

To my great relief the capybara wasn't there! He was crouched in a clump of the tropical plants, as still as a stone, with his eyes tightly closed. The only sign of life was the fact he was sitting up.

I wondered what had caused his sudden flare of anger. Or had it been sudden? Maybe his resentment of human creatures had been growing for some time, ever since he had been banished from the family circle in the evenings.

Despite his blunt clumsy appearance he was a highly sensitive animal. To be accepted as one of us for most of the summer then abruptly rejected and left in a lonely pen must have been bewildering. For all Capy knew, he was being punished, and for no reason. This might have aroused a deep resentment which finally exploded in anger, and unfortunately Tommy was there when it happened. I was still puzzling over the matter when Margaret and Steve returned with news of Tommy.

The scalp wound had been painful, but not serious. After it was treated and stitched the doctor assured them it would leave only a small scar which would be covered nicely by Tommy's thick shock of hair.

Now it was time to worry about Capy's condition. He hadn't changed position in the slightest for more than an hour. We called to him hoping he might respond in some way, but there wasn't so much as a turn of the head or the twitch of an ear. There he remained without moving, his eyes tightly closed all through the afternoon.

Just before sundown we carried the limp and helpless capy-bara back to his pen and Margaret covered him with a blanket, knowing that shock victims must be kept warm. Then we slid his cardboard house over him and left him there, with the awful feeling that this might be the end of Capy.

Early the next morning, as much as we dreaded it, Margaret and I went out to the pen for a look. Steve was already there offering Capy food and water, but he showed no interest whatsoever. He was just as we had left him the night before with the blanket undisturbed. The fact that he was still breathing was the only hopeful sign.

On the second morning his condition remained the same. For all we could see he hadn't stirred from the one position. He gave no sign of improving all through the afternoon and on into the evening when Tommy Hall telephoned to find out how Capy was doing.

"My head doesn't hurt anymore," he said, "and I'm not mad at Capy. I hope he gets well."

And Capy *did* get well. On the third morning he was able to sit up and take a few nibbles of food and drink some water. Within a week his appetite had improved until he was eating at top speed and feeling as good as new.

Meanwhile Tommy Hall who lived a few miles away had become something of a celebrity in his neighborhood. The capybara scar was his badge of distinction. After all, not many boys in Los Angeles, or anywhere else in the country for that matter, can boast of being bitten by a capybara. And to top off Tommy's week of glory, a CAPYBARA BITES BOY! column appeared in the newspaper.

Of course we didn't want any other small boys becoming famous on account of Capy and we began pondering the problem of what to do with our rambunctious rodent.

I suggested we donate the capybara to the Los Angeles Zoo, but Margaret objected.

"That's like sending Capy to prison," she said. "Why don't we ship him back to South America with instructions that he be returned to the jungle?"

"Not a bad idea," I said, "if we could be sure the instructions would be carried out. Somewhere along the line he might end up in the wrong hands. Capybaras are considered good eating by many people down in that country."

Margaret had another idea. "Why don't we take the trip ourselves? Then we could make sure he gets back to the jungle."

55

"That's the only sure way," I agreed, "but for all we know Capy wouldn't last a minute in the jungle. His animal instincts for survival may have been dulled after spending most of his life in captivity. He might assume that the jungle is nothing more than one enormous backyard, the rivers and swamps just so many harmless swimming pools, completely unaware of the crocodiles, jaguars and giant anacondas lurking everywhere.

"If we should turn him loose in the jungle he might walk straight into the jaws of a prowling jaguar. It would be something to wonder and worry about long afterward."

We were still puzzling over the problem when Bill returned from Mexico.

After hearing about Tommy Hall and what a big problem our rebellious rodent had become, Bill reluctantly agreed that Capy must go. What to do with him was still a puzzling question, and we hoped Bill might come up with a happy solution. We discussed the problem for days, considering every possible angle, only to arrive at the one inevitable conclusion — Capy must go to the zoo.

One morning Bill carried his kicking, squealing, big rodent out to his jeep — a wildly desperate struggle all the way. Once inside the car Capy settled down to gaze calmly out a window, apparently resigned to whatever his fate might be.

Then as the jeep wheeled out of the driveway and headed
down the road, Margaret burst into tears.

"It's not goodbye forever," I reminded her. "After all, the
zoo is only a half-hour drive from here."

And since that day we have taken that drive many a time
and brought Capy many a sack of freshly cut grass. On one of
these visits we were horrified to find our capybara sharing a
pen and swimming pool with a pair of huge hippos.

It seemed to us that the zoo had made a mistake, but after checking with one of the attendants, we were reassured that the capy and the hippos got along fine.

"In fact," the man said with a chuckle, "I've even seen Capy walking around on their backs."

With this cheering news the attendant left us. If Capy could walk on the hippos there seemed to be nothing more to worry about.

Margaret called "Capyboppy! Capyboppy!" which brought him tweetling happily up to the fence, and I tossed our bundle of grass over to him.

Just as Capy settled down to enjoy his treat the male hippopotamus caught the scent of the fresh greenery and came plodding across the pen.

We watched anxiously as Capy stood his ground chomping away at the grass, with one eye on the approaching hippo. For a tense moment they were nose to nose. Then with a pitiful squeak Capy backed away to watch his precious grass disappear in one big "WHUFFLE!"

Now we feared Capy might starve if he must share all his meals with these bigmouthed blimps, and we couldn't very well leave the zoo with this worry on our minds.

There was a park bench just across the walk from the pen and we sat there to watch until feeding time. By then the hippos had retired to the swimming pool, floating there like two blubbery islands. So Capy was left to eat alone, and he plunked himself down in the feed box for a bountiful feast of lettuce, cabbage, carrots, and celery.

We should have known better than to worry about our big rodent getting enough to eat. And as we left the zoo I wondered if we shouldn't worry more about the poor hippos. If anyone ever goes hungry in that pen it won't be Capyboppy.